Australia

by Tracey Boraas

Content Consultant:
Dr. Patty O'Brien, Professor of Australian History
Center for Australian and New Zealand Studies
Georgetown University, Washington, DC

Reading Consultant:
Dr. Robert Miller, Professor of Special Education,
Minnesota State University, Mankato

Bridgestone Books
an imprint of Capstone Press
Mankato, Minnesota

Bridgestone Books are published by Capstone Press
151 Good Counsel Drive, P.O. Box 669, Mankato, Minnesota 56002
http://www.capstone-press.com

Library of Congress Cataloging-in-Publication Data
Boraas, Tracey.
    Australia / by Tracey Boraas.
    p. cm.—(Countries and cultures)
    Includes bibliographical references and index.
    ISBN-10: 0-7368-1075-7 (hardcover)
    ISBN-13: 978-0-7368-6949-2 (softcover pbk.)
    ISBN-10: 0-7368-6949-2 (softcover pbk.)
1. Australia—Juvenile literature. [1. Australia.] I. Title. II. Series.
DU96 .B67 2002
994—dc21   2001005129

Summary: An introduction to the geography, history, economy, culture,
    and people of Australia.

Editorial Credits
Gillia M. Olson, editor; Heather Kindseth, cover designer and interior layout
    designer; Heidi Meyer, interior illustrator; Alta Schaffer, photo researcher

Photo Credits
AFP/Torsten Blackwood/CORBIS, 33; Brian Rogers/Visuals Unlimited, 12;
Capstone Press/Gary Sundermeyer, 49; CORBIS, cover (left), 1 (left, right), 4,
11, 15, 20, 29, 45, 47, 51, 55, 56, 63; Digital Stock, 1 (middle), 18, 19;
Hulton/Archive Photos, 23, 25, 26; Index Stock Imagery/Lonnie Duka, 34;
Index Stock Imagery/Chad Ehlers, 42; Kay Shaw, 53; Michael S.
Yamashita/CORBIS, 38; One Mile Up, Inc., 57 (both); Paul A.
Souders/CORBIS, 31; Pictor, cover (right); Tom Till, 8

Artistic Effects
Artville/Jeff Burke and Lorraine Triolo; Corbis; Digital Stock; PhotoDisc, Inc.

1 2 3 4 5 6 07 06 05 04 03 02

Contents

Fast Facts about Australia

Official name: Commonwealth of Australia
Location: Oceania (between the Pacific Ocean and
the Indian Ocean)
Bordering waters: Pacific Ocean, Indian Ocean
National population: 19,164,620
Capital city and population: Canberra (278,894)
Major cities and populations: Sydney (3,664,000),
Melbourne (3,187,000), Brisbane (1,591,000),
Perth (1,313,000), Adelaide (1,063,000)

Chapter 1

Explore Australia

More than 500,000 years ago, coral skeletons began hardening in the Pacific Ocean along the northeastern coast of Australia. These fossils form the base of Australia's most famous attraction, the Great Barrier Reef. This system of coral reefs stretches about 1,250 miles (2,010 kilometers) along Australia's northeastern coast. Live corals that grow on top of the skeletons are a variety of colors, including blue, green, purple, red, and yellow.

The Great Barrier Reef ecosystem contains a huge variety of animals and plants. More than 1,500 fish species find food and shelter on the Great Barrier Reef. Crabs, giant clams, and sea turtles also make the reef their home. Colorful, jellylike sea anemones attach to the coral reefs.

Millions of tourists visit the Great Barrier Reef each year. They snorkel, fish, and even walk among the reefs. But careless tourists can damage the reef

◀ Corals on the Great Barrier Reef grow into a variety of shapes.

system by removing or killing animals and plants. Run-off chemicals from the cities and farmlands along the coast can kill coral and other sea life. The Great Barrier Reef Park Authority manages and tries to stop damage to the reef system. Australians want the reef system to be around for people to enjoy in the future.

The Country Continent

Australia is the only country in the world that also is a continent. Australia is located completely within the Southern Hemisphere. The Pacific Ocean lies to the north and east of Australia while the Indian Ocean lies west and south of the country. Mainland Asia is about 2,000 miles (3,200 kilometers) across the waters to the northwest.

Australia is the sixth largest country in the world. It covers about 3 million square miles (7.8 million square kilometers). Australia has about 19 million people. In comparison, the United States covers about 3.7 million square miles (9.6 million square kilometers) and has a population of about 273 million.

Australia is known for its beautiful scenery, natural resources, and friendly people. It is a highly industrialized nation, but it still depends on agriculture and mining for much of its wealth. Australians enjoy modern conveniences and have a high standard of living.

Indonesia

*Indian
Ocean*

*Pacific
Ocean*

Northern Territory

Queensland

Western Australia

Australia

Brisban ●

South Australia

Perth ●

New South Wales

Australian
Capital Territory →⊗ ● Sydney
Canberra

Adelaide ●

Victoria

Indian Ocean

●Melbourne

N

W   E

S

Tasmania

*Pacific
Ocean*

Scale
Miles
0   150   300   450   600

0   200   400   600   800
Kilometers

Geopolitical Map of Australia

KEY
⊗ CAPITAL
● CITIES

Fast Facts about Australia's Land

Area: 2,967,893 square miles (7,686,850 square kilometers)
Latitude and longitude of geographic center: 27 degrees south latitude, 133 degrees east longitude
Highest elevation: Mount Kosciusko, 7310 feet (2,229 meters)
Lowest elevation: Lake Eyre, 52 feet (15 meters) below sea level
States and Territories: New South Wales, Queensland, South Australia, Western Australia, Victoria, Tasmania, Northern Territory, Australian Capital Territory

Chapter 2

The Land, Climate, and Wildlife

Australia's position south of the equator makes its seasons opposite of those in the Northern Hemisphere. The northern third of Australia has warm, tropical weather all year with only two seasons. Winter is the dry season and runs from May through October. The wet summer lasts from November through April.

Southern Australia has four separate seasons that include warm, dry summers and cool, wet winters. Temperatures in the region rarely dip below freezing. But some areas in the mountains and far to the south receive occasional frost and snowfall.

Nearly one-third of Australia is desert that receives less than 10 inches (25 centimeters) of rain each year. Most of Australia receives annual rainfall of less than 20 inches (51 centimeters).

Australia can be divided into three major regions according to land features. These regions are the

◄ Elabana Falls' dense foliage thrives in the rain forest climate of northeastern Australia.

Eastern Highlands, the Central Lowlands, and the Western Plateau.

The Eastern Highlands

The Eastern Highlands region stretches from northeastern Cape York Peninsula to the southern coast of Tasmania. Tasmania is an island located about 150 miles (240 kilometers) from the mainland. Low plains, sandy beaches, and rocky cliffs stretch along the coast of the Highlands.

The Eastern Highlands region contains most of Australia's people. Southeastern Australia, from Brisbane to Melbourne, is the most heavily populated part of the country. Four of Australia's five largest cities are located there.

The Great Dividing Range separates the Eastern Highlands region from the rest of Australia. This range consists of high plateaus, hills, and low mountains. Rich soil on some of the Highland plateaus support crops. Grasslands and forests cover other plateaus. The Australian Alps are located in the southern part of the Eastern Highlands. Mount Kosciusko, Australia's highest point, rises 7,310 feet (2,228 meters) in the Alps' Snowy Mountain range.

The region's climate varies. The northeastern coast is the hottest and wettest part of the country. This area commonly receives up to 150 inches (381 centimeters)

▼ Most Australians live in the Eastern Highlands region. Sydney, shown below, is Australia's largest city.

▲ The Central Lowlands contain many dry lakes, which often are covered in a white, salty crust.

12

of rain each year. The southern part of the region has milder temperatures. Sydney, a city on the southeastern coast, averages about 70 degrees Fahrenheit (21 degrees Celsius) throughout the year. Sydney receives 48 inches (122 centimeters) of rain each year.

The Central Lowlands

The Central Lowlands region lies to the west of the Highlands. This largely flat area contains Australia's lowest elevations. Lake Eyre is the lowest point in Australia at 52 feet (16 meters) below sea level. It is found in the west-central part of the Lowlands. Lake Eyre is one of the world's largest lakes. But it usually is dry and covered in a white, salty crust. If the area receives enough rain, the lake fills with water. This type of rainfall only happens about every 50 years.

Much of the Lowlands region is too dry and hot for crops. The Simpson Desert lies along the region's western edge. Occasional rain fills the Lowlands region's usually dry riverbeds. Most of the land, which is covered with coarse grass or shrubs, is used to graze livestock. Farmers can grow wheat in the southern part of the Central Lowlands where rain is more frequent.

The southern part of the region contains most of its population. Australia's fourth largest city, Adelaide, is located here. Many people also live along Encounter Bay, the end of the Murray River. The Murray forms part of the border of the state of Victoria. The Darling River, Australia's longest river, empties into the Murray River.

The Western Plateau

The Western Plateau region covers two-thirds of Australia. This region is mostly flat, but includes low mountains such as the MacDonnell and Musgrave ranges. The Gibson Desert, Great Sandy Desert, and Great Victoria Desert cover the central part of the Western Plateau. Livestock graze on grass and shrubs along the outer areas of the deserts. Sparsely populated areas in this region and the Central Lowlands are called the Outback.

Most of the Western Plateau's population and farmland are located to the north and southwest, where rainfall is heaviest. Perth, the region's largest city, is located in the southern part of the region along the west coast. Farmers grow grain on the Nullarbor Plain, which runs about 400 miles (640 kilometers) along the southern edge of the Western Plateau region.

In Australia's Northern Territory, an enormous rock suddenly rises from the sandy plains. Uluru Rock stands 1,100 feet (335 meters) high in the middle of flat, level land. Uluru Rock, formerly known as Ayers Rock, means "The Great Pebble" in the Aboriginal language. Uluru Rock is more than 1.5 miles (2.4 kilometers) long, 1 mile (1.6 kilometers) wide, and 5 miles (8 kilometers) around at its base.

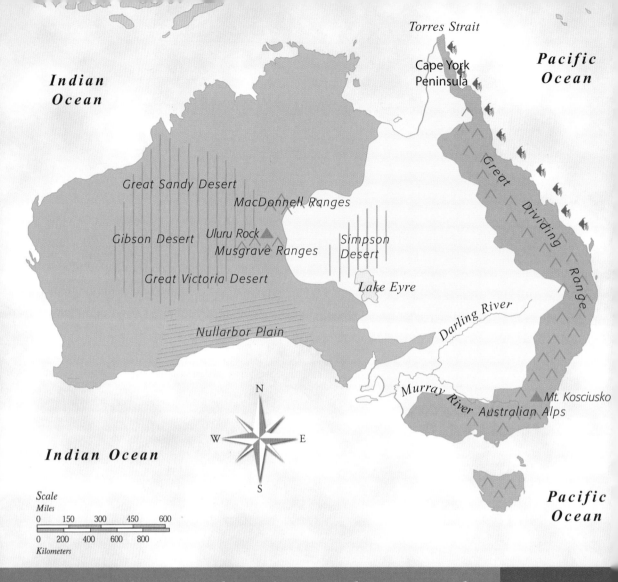

Torres Strait

Cape York
Peninsula

*Pacific
Ocean*

*Indian
Ocean*

Great Sandy Desert

MacDonnell Ranges

Gibson Desert   Uluru Rock
Musgrave Ranges

Great Victoria Desert

Simpson
Desert

Lake Eyre

Great Dividing Range

Nullarbor Plain

Darling River

Murray River   Mt. Kosciusko
Australian Alps

N
W   E
S

Indian Ocean

*Pacific
Ocean*

Scale
Miles
0   150   300   450   600
0   200   400   600   800
Kilometers

Australia's Land Regions and Topography

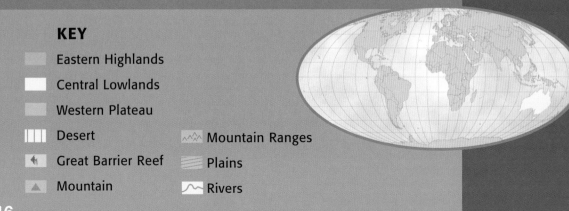

KEY

Eastern Highlands

Central Lowlands

Western Plateau

|||| Desert

Great Barrier Reef

Mountain

Mountain Ranges

Plains

Rivers

Wildlife

Australia is home to many types of animals not found anywhere else in the world. The country has 150 species of marsupials such as kangaroos, koalas, Tasmanian devils, and wombats. Marsupials give birth to tiny offspring that mature in a pouch on the mother's stomach. The koala makes its home on the East Coast of Australia. This marsupial eats only the leaves of Australia's eucalyptus trees. The Tasmanian devil lurks in the dense forest of Tasmania. This black and white marsupial can grow to 4 feet (1.2 meters) long with a 1-foot (30-centimeter) tail. This vicious animal has sharp claws and teeth.

Australia is home to nearly 700 species of birds. Black swans are native only to Australia. The country's best-known bird, the kookaburra, is a member of the kingfisher family. This thick-bodied bird has a large beak and bushy feathers on its head. Close to 60 kinds of cockatoos, parakeets, and other parrots live in Australia. Three large flightless birds, the emu, cassowary, and ostrich, also live in the country.

Lizards and snakes make their homes in Australia. The poisonous taipan and the tiger snake are two of Australia's native, deadly snakes. Most of the country's other 140 species of snakes also are poisonous. But all 370 species of Australia's lizards are harmless. Some species of barking and frilled lizards are found only in Australia.

Australia now is home to animals that are not native to the country. Thousands of years ago, Aborigines settling in the country brought along the dingo. Today, this type of wild dog is the main animal of prey across the Australian countryside. European settlers brought cattle, sheep, goats, horses, pigs, deer, foxes, and rabbits to Australia.

Many of Australia's animals are in danger of dying out. For example, cats and foxes, brought by settlers, prey on native animals such as the bilby and wallaby. The population of freshwater crocodiles has decreased due to illegal hunting. As wildlife areas are cleared for agriculture and forestry, many more animals lose their natural living areas.

dingo

Australians are working to protect endangered animals. Laws make it illegal to hunt or kill them. The government has set aside wildlife areas where animals are protected and can live safely.

Kangaroos

The kangaroo is one of Australia's national animals. The red kangaroo lives in the deserts and dry grasslands of central Australia. Gray kangaroos live in southern and eastern Australia. Usually, kangaroos stay in small groups of mothers and joeys, but they sometimes gather in large groups called mobs.

Kangaroos use their large, powerful hind legs to hop as fast as 30 miles (48 kilometers) an hour. A kangaroo can leap over objects 6 feet (1.8 meters) high. The kangaroo's long tail provides balance.

Kangaroos are marsupials. They give birth to joeys. The undeveloped joey is only 1 inch (2.5 centimeters) long at birth. It continues to grow in the mother's pouch for six to eight months.

▲ Red kangaroos live in Australian grasslands. Kangaroos keep their joey in their pouch for six to eight months.

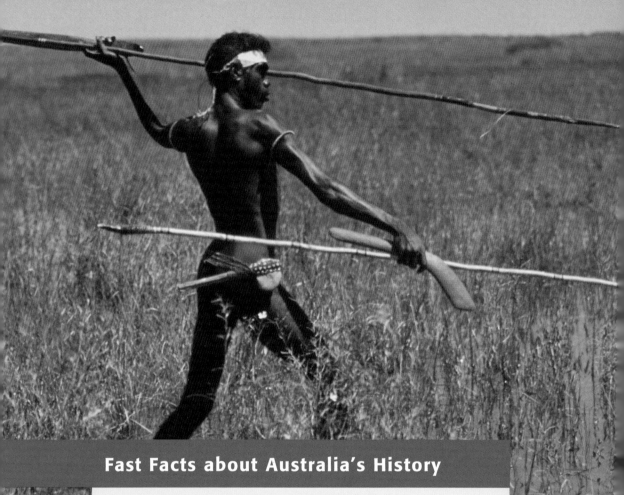

Fast Facts about Australia's History

First European claim: 1770

Claimant: James Cook

Constitution date: July 9, 1900; effective January 1, 1901

National holiday: Australia Day, January 26

Current type of government: Constitutional monarchy

Head of state: British monarch

Head of government: prime minister

Chapter 3

Australia's History and Government

Aboriginal peoples arrived in Australia about 50,000 years ago. They probably came from Southeast Asia. The Aborigines were hunters and gatherers. They followed the animals they hunted, and gathered roots and other plants to eat. The Torres Strait Islanders were another, smaller group of people who occupied islands near the Torres Strait, north of Australia. These people developed a separate culture.

European Discovery

In the 1500s, European explorers began searching for a continent that they believed was south of Asia. They called this area Terra Australis Incognita, or Unknown Southern Land. Early explorers found the island of New Guinea northeast of Australia. But the continent lay undiscovered about 100 miles (160 kilometers) to the south.

◀ This Aboriginal man hunts in a marsh. The Aborigines have practiced their culture's traditions longer than any other known group.

Spanish and Dutch explorers continued to search the area. In 1606, Spanish explorer Luis Vaez de Torres sailed through a strait in between New Guinea and Australia. It was later named Torres Strait after him.

Also in 1606, Dutch navigator Willem Jansz became the first European known to land in Australia. Jansz thought he had sailed to a coast of New Guinea. He actually had landed on the west coast of Cape York Peninsula in northeastern Australia.

From 1642 to 1643, a Dutch sea captain named Abel Janszoon Tasman sailed completely around Australia without sighting the continent. He instead found an island south of Australia's eastern coast that he called Van Diemen's Land. The island later was renamed Tasmania to honor Tasman.

Early European explorers did not like the dry and barren land that they found in Australia. It offered no gold, riches, or anything else Europeans valued. Then in 1770, James Cook of the British Navy explored Australia's fertile east coast. Cook claimed the area for Great Britain and named it New South Wales.

Prison Colonies

In the 1780s, Great Britain's prisons were very overcrowded. Government officials decided to use Australia as a colony to house criminals. This practice was called transportation. In 1786, Arthur Phillip was

This illustration shows a criminal settlement on Norfolk Island in New South Wales. Nearly 160,000 convicts were sent to prison colonies in Australia.

appointed to establish a prison colony in New South Wales and serve as its governor.

On January 18, 1788, the first ship of British convicts landed at Botany Bay on Australia's East Coast. A total of 11 ships arrived carrying about 570 male and 160 female criminals. Other passengers included about 200 British guards and their families. On January 26, these people moved a few miles (kilometers) north and founded Australia's first European settlement at present-day Sydney, Australia.

Great Britain soon set up more prison colonies in Australia. The guards established community farms to provide food for all the people in the colony. Convicts cleared and farmed the land, and built houses.

In the 1790s, the British government began to give land to guards and to convicts who had completed their prison terms. Many of these landowners raised sheep and exported the wool to Britain. Before long, noncriminal settlers began arriving from Great Britain.

The arrival of the prisoners and guards in 1788 marked the beginning of what would become known as the Frontier War. During the next 150 years, white settlers fought with Aboriginal peoples over land. Thousands of Aboriginal peoples were killed during the Frontier War. Many Aboriginal peoples were forced onto reservations. Aboriginal children also were taken away from their parents.

Continued Exploration

Australian settlers did not know if they were living on an island or if they were connected to another continent. The country's southern and northern coastlines were not charted. Between 1801 and 1803, British navigator Matthew Flinders sailed around the continent, proving that Australia actually was one large landmass. By the 1820s, the continent was known as Australia.

When white settlers first arrived in Australia, they wanted to maintain peace with the Aborigines. This 1816 illustration shows that Aborigines and Europeans were supposed to be equal under the law.

People began settling other areas of Australia. Prison colonies were established in Tasmania, leading to its status as a colony in 1825. A sea captain named Charles Fremantle landed on Australia's southwest coast in 1829. He claimed this land and established the colony of Western Australia that same year. Also in 1829, Charles Sturt explored southern Australia near

▼ Prospectors in Australia's gold fields panned for nuggets.

present-day Adelaide. By 1836, settlers established South Australia in this territory.

Success with Sheep and Gold

Australians were making large profits from wool trade with Great Britain. Some sheep farmers moved to southern New South Wales. They settled on the rich grazing lands south of the Murray River, founding the city of Melbourne. In 1851, Britain made this part of New South Wales a separate colony called Victoria.

In 1851, miners discovered gold in New South Wales and Victoria. Thousands of gold seekers from overseas rushed to Australia. The colony's population grew from 400,000 to more than 1.1 million. Many who came searching for gold settled in Australia.

Self-Government

In the early 1850s, Great Britain stopped sending criminals to the eastern colonies of Australia. The number of free settlers in the Australian colonies increased. In 1859, Great Britain created a separate colony called Queensland in northeastern Australia.

Australia's settlers wanted the power to govern themselves. Great Britain granted all colonies self-government by 1859, with the exception of Western Australia. Britain maintained control of some powers, including foreign affairs and defense. Western Australia remained a destination for transported criminals. Britain finally ended this practice in 1868. Western Australia gained self-government in 1890.

By the 1890s, many Australians wanted to unite their colonies into a single nation with one government. During 1897 and 1898, Australians wrote a constitution. Great Britain approved it in 1900.

On January 1, 1901, the Commonwealth of Australia became an independent nation, and the colonies became states. The Northern Territory was an exception. The Northern Territory gained self-government in 1978. Melbourne became the temporary home for the federal government. In 1908, the government selected Canberra as the permanent capital.

The War Years

During World War I (1914–1918), Australian and New Zealand troops fought together as the Australian and New Zealand Army Corps (ANZACS). These troops teamed with the Allied Forces of Great Britain, France, and the United States against Germany, Austria, and Hungary.

Australia again allied with Great Britain against Germany when World War II (1939–1945) started. At first, Australian forces fought against German and Italian troops in Greece, Crete, and northern Africa. But in March of 1942, Japanese troops allied with Germany tried to invade Australia. Australia spent the rest of the war keeping Japanese forces out of Australia.

The end of World War II brought changes to the country's "white Australia" policy toward immigration. Previously, Australia had barred most people from countries other than Great Britain and Ireland from becoming citizens. After World War II, the government allowed immigrants

from all over Europe to come to Australia. Australia slowly loosened its immigration policies even further. Today, Australia welcomes immigrants from around the world.

Australia began to take a more active role in world affairs after World War II. It joined the United Nations (UN) in 1945. Australia contributed to the UN forces that fought in the Korean War (1950–1953). Australian troops also assisted the United States in the Vietnam

War (1954–1975). In 1999, Australia led the UN forces in East Timor, part of an island in Southeast Asia.

Modern Government

Australia's government has three levels—local, state or territorial, and national. Local governments usually manage community services. Australian states and territories make laws regarding issues such as education, law enforcement, and health services. The national government makes laws that affect the entire country.

Australia's national government is made up of the legislative, executive, and judicial branches. It is a constitutional monarchy. Australia recognizes Great Britain's monarch as the head of state and executive branch. A governor general represents the British monarch in Australia. But he or she has little power. The governor general mainly serves as a symbol of the tie between the two countries.

The executive branch also includes the prime minister and cabinet. The prime minister is the head of Australia's government. The majority party in the House of Representatives appoints the prime minister. The majority party also selects a cabinet, which is made up of members of Parliament. The cabinet oversees government departments and makes government policies.

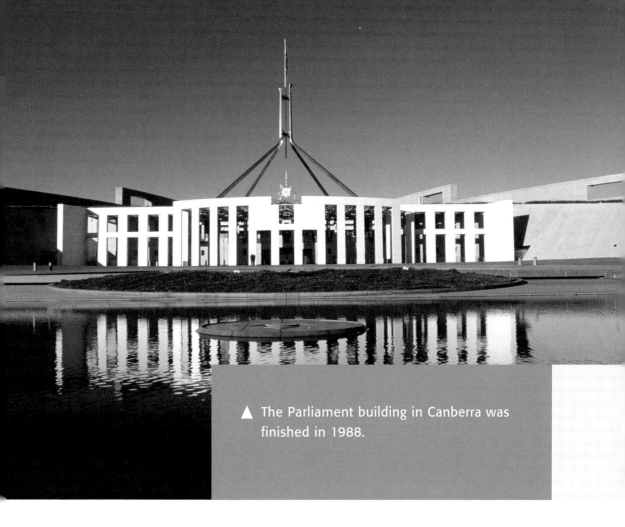

▲ The Parliament building in Canberra was finished in 1988.

The legislative branch, or Parliament, makes laws. It consists of the Senate and the House of Representatives. The Senate has 76 members. State senators are elected to six-year terms. Territorial senators are elected to three-year terms. The House of Representatives has 148 members. Representatives are elected for three-year terms. All Australians 18 years of age or older are required to vote in federal and state elections.

Australia's court system makes up the judicial branch. The High Court is Australia's highest court. The judicial branch also includes other federal courts that decide such issues as criminal and family law.

Political Challenges

Australians continue to try to make Australia a fair place for everyone. Aboriginal peoples were not considered citizens until 1967. During the 1990s, the government created the Aboriginal and Torres Strait Islander Commission. This organization seeks to represent Aboriginal peoples in government policies that affect them.

In 1993, the Native Title Act gave Aboriginal peoples the right to make claims on tribal land in Australia. Farmers and miners who live on possible tribal land do not want to lose it. The government passed an amendment to the Native Title Act in 1997. This amendment makes it clearer what areas can be claimed as tribal lands.

Australia also faces the challenge of becoming a completely independent country. Many Australians want a president to replace the British monarch as head of state. Australia held a referendum on November 6, 1999. This vote asked if Australia's governor general should be replaced with a president elected by a two-thirds

◄ Aboriginal elder Kevin Buzzacott (wearing the red sash) finishes a peace trek to Sydney during the 2000 Olympics.

majority vote in Parliament. This change would make Australia a republic rather than a constitutional monarchy. A slim majority of Australians voted to keep the current system. Some experts believe Australians wanted a president elected by the people, rather than by Parliament. This fact may have caused many people to vote against the referendum. Further referendums may be held on this issue.

Fast Facts about Australia's Economy

System of weights and measures: metric
Major types of industry: mining, industrial and transportation equipment, food processing, chemicals, steel
Major natural resources/minerals: coal, iron ore, tin, zinc, copper, lead, bauxite, uranium
Major agricultural products: wheat, barley, cattle, sheep
Major types of manufactured products: transportation equipment, chemicals
Chief exports: coal, meat, wool, alumina, iron ore, wheat
Chief imports: computers and office machines, petroleum

Chapter 4

Australia's Economy

Australia's economy is flourishing. Most developed countries have built strong economies from the export of manufactured products. But Australia's wealth came from the farming and mining industries. Australia continues to depend on agriculture and mining products to provide the country with its major exports.

Mining and Manufacturing

During the 1800s, Australia began to develop its rich mineral resources and began exporting copper, gold, lead, silver, tin, and zinc. Today, minerals and other raw materials account for about 45 percent of the money from Australia's exports. Coal and gold are Australia's leading mineral exports. Australians also mine large amounts of uranium, diamonds, lead, copper, iron ore, nickel, silver, zinc, and bauxite.

◀ Large Australian goldmines like this one near Kalgoorlie contribute to the country's mineral wealth.

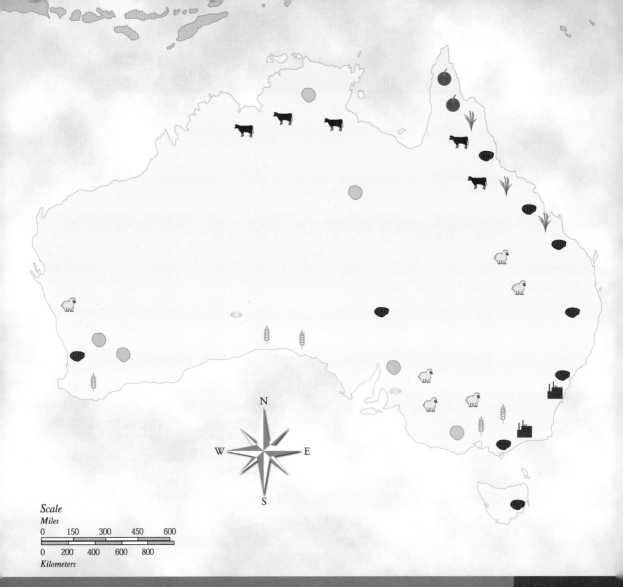

Australia's Industries and Natural Resources

KEY

- 🐄 Beef
- 🪨 Coal
- 🍎 Fruits
- ⚪ Gold
- 🏭 Manufacturing
- ⬭ Opals
- 🐑 Sheep
- 🌾 Sugarcane
- 🌾 Wheat

Scale
Miles
0   150   300   450   600

0   200   400   600   800
Kilometers

Australian mines produce the world's best-quality opals, which are pearl-like gemstones.

Mining is difficult and expensive in Australia. Valuable minerals are frequently located in areas that are far from towns. Roads or railroads must be built so miners can travel to these mining sites. The mining industry employs about 1 percent of the country's workforce.

Nearly half of Australia's mining industry is owned or controlled by foreigners. Businesses from other countries use their own money to develop mining sites. In return, they receive part of the money that is made from the mines.

Australia's main manufacturing states are New South Wales and Victoria. Workers there produce processed foods, textiles, clothing, and shoes. Australian manufacturers also make household appliances, metals, chemicals, paper, and automobiles. A major part of Australia's manufacturing industry includes processing farm and mineral products for export. Manufactured goods make up about 35 percent of exports. The manufacturing industry employs about 22 percent of Australia's workers.

Agriculture

Farming is vital to Australia's economy. Nearly 60 percent of the country is farmland, but farmers can grow crops on only 10 percent of this land. Most of the other farmland is used for livestock grazing.

Australian farmers produce most of the food needed by the people in the country. Farm products such as meat, wool, and wheat make up about 20 percent of Australia's exports. But this huge industry employs only 5 percent of the country's workers.

Wool and beef are the country's major farm products. Farmers raise cattle and sheep on large ranches, called stations. Australia is the world's largest producer and exporter of wool. More than half of Australia's wool comes from the stations in New South Wales and Western Australia. The country also is a leading producer and exporter of beef. More than half of Australia's beef cattle are raised on stations in Queensland and New South Wales.

Farmers grow many other crops to feed the country's population and to export. They grow wheat in New South Wales and southwestern Australia.

◀ A farm hand feeds lambs with a bottle at a sheep station in the Outback.

Farmers grow sugarcane along the eastern coast of Queensland. Fruits such as bananas and pineapples thrive in northern Australia's wet, tropical climate. In contrast, Australia's hot, drier areas are perfect for vineyards. Farmers in all states can grow fruits such as apples and pears. Barley, poultry, cotton, and dairy products also are produced on Australia's farms.

Many farmers also are raising indigenous plants and animals. Some harvest macadamia nuts. Others raise kangaroos and emus for meat.

Service and Tourism

More than 70 percent of Australians work in the service industry. They hold jobs in hospitals, schools, government agencies, stores, hotels, restaurants, and banks.

The tourism industry also contributes largely to Australia's economy. About 4 million tourists visit Australia each year to see the Great Barrier Reef, the Australian Alps, and other attractions. However, Australia's distance from other countries blocks the growth of its tourism industry. Most tourists come from countries near Australia, such as New Zealand, Japan, and countries in Southeast Asia.

20 cent coin

50 cent coin

10 cent coin

Australia's currency is the Australian dollar. One dollar equals 100 cents.

Currency exchange rates change every day. In the early 2000s, about 1.71 Australian dollars equaled 1.00 U.S. dollar, and about 1.16 Australian dollars equaled 1.00 Canadian dollar.

5 dollar bill
(front & back)

1 dollar coin

41

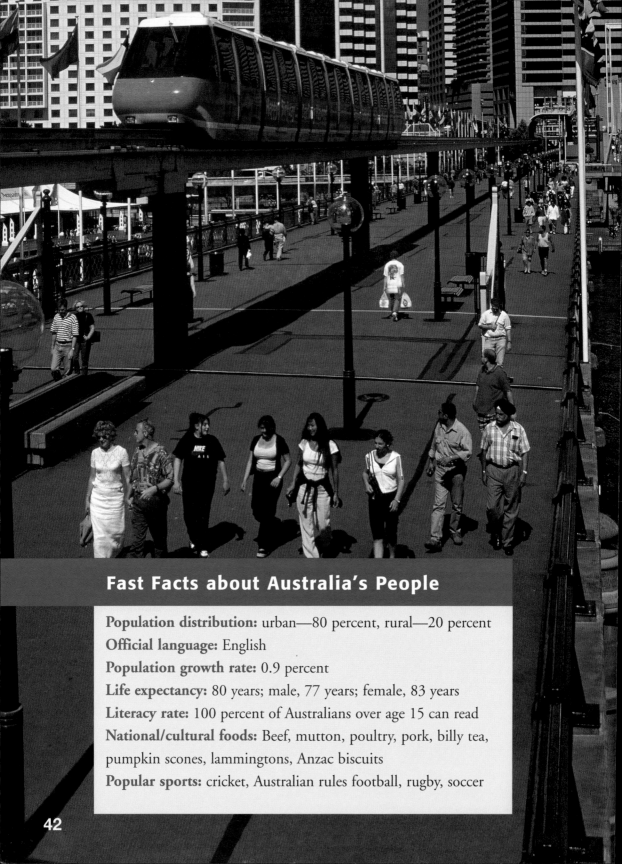

Fast Facts about Australia's People

Population distribution: urban—80 percent, rural—20 percent

Official language: English

Population growth rate: 0.9 percent

Life expectancy: 80 years; male, 77 years; female, 83 years

Literacy rate: 100 percent of Australians over age 15 can read

National/cultural foods: Beef, mutton, poultry, pork, billy tea, pumpkin scones, lammingtons, Anzac biscuits

Popular sports: cricket, Australian rules football, rugby, soccer

Chapter 5

People, Culture, and Daily Life

Australians call themselves Aussies. Aussies are known to be relaxed and friendly people. Most Australians are middle class, share similar values, and have a fairly high level of education.

Cultural Diversity

Three hundred years ago, 750,000 Aborigines lived in Australia. Today, only 257,000 Aborigines live in the country. Most of these Aborigines are of mixed Caucasian and Aboriginal background.

Ninety-two percent of Australians have European backgrounds. Either they or their ancestors moved to Australia from Europe. Most of these people originally came from Great Britain or Ireland.

Australia has a large immigrant population. Almost 20 percent of all Australians were born in other countries. After 1945, immigrants from southern

◀ Diverse people can be seen walking along the Darling Harbor pier in Sydney.

European countries such as Greece and Italy came to Australia. Other immigrants have come from New Zealand and Southeast Asia. Asian peoples make up 7 percent of Australia's population.

English is Australia's official language. Australian English differs from British and American English. Settlers needed words to describe unfamiliar animals and plants in their new home. They used some Aboriginal words such as "kangaroo" and "koala." Settlers in Australia's interior also invented words such as "Outback."

City and Rural Life

Nearly 80 percent of Australians live in southeastern cities. Most other people live along the northeastern and the southwestern coasts. These areas receive enough rainfall to support a large population. People in inner city areas often live in apartments. Those living on the outskirts of cities often own their own home, because there is plenty of space for houses.

About 15 percent of the Australian population lives in rural areas called the bush. The vast, dry interior regions also are called the Outback. The Outback is too dry to support a large population. It consists of huge areas of grazing land, widely scattered farm settlements, and mining towns.

▼ Australians ride horses in the Outback, also called the bush.

Most farms in the Outback are cattle or sheep stations. Some of these stations cover more than 1,000 square miles (2,600 square kilometers) and are located more than 100 miles (160 kilometers) from the nearest town. Life on these stations usually is very isolated. Travel by automobile may be impossible in areas where there are no paved roads. Families may travel to town only a few times each year. Some farm families keep a small airplane for transportation. Although the isolation can be difficult, the majority of these families live comfortably.

Aboriginal Life

Many Aborigines live in the Australian Outback. Here, tribal communities practice traditional ways of life. However, some young Aborigines choose to live in cities. They often face discrimination based on their skin color or their beliefs.

Aborigines generally make less money than other Australians. They often have less education, poorer housing, and poorer healthcare.

Education

Australia's education system is very successful. Nearly 100 percent of the Australian population can read and write. In Australia, 75 percent of children go to free public schools run by states or territories. Other children pay a fee to attend private schools. Most states and territories require children to go to school from ages 6 to 15.

Children in the Outback receive their education at home because they often live far away from schools.

Learn to Speak Strine

Australians speak an English dialect that they call "Strine." The word Strine comes from the Australian's way of pronouncing words as in "Au-strine." They pronounce words by keeping the tongue low in the mouth. For example, the long "a" sound is pronounced as a long "i." The word day is pronounced "die."

Basic Phrases:

friend—mate	farewell or goodbye—cop you later, toroo
afternoon—arvo	good morning/good day—g'day
thank you—ta	sheep—jumbuck

Correspondence schools allow students to receive and turn in their assignments by mail. Some students go to broadcasting centers where they can communicate over two-way radios with teachers. This type of education is called "school of the air."

Religion

The Australian Constitution protects religious freedom for its citizens. Australians can practice any religion they wish. Most Australians are Christians. Anglicans and Roman Catholics each account for 26 percent of the population. Another 24 percent of the population practices other Christian denominations.

About 11 percent of Australia's people practice religions such as Judaism, Islam, and Aboriginal faiths. Aborigines practice a religion in which plants, animals, and land features are sacred.

Australian Food

Food in Australia reflects its cultural diversity. Immigrants bring their traditional cooking methods to Australia. Asian, Italian, and Greek foods are popular.

In the past, Australians ate meat with every meal. As farmers, they ate large breakfasts to keep up energy for hard daily labor.

Today, Australian dishes vary widely. Many eat cereal or toast for breakfast. Australians often eat a

Make Lammingtons

Lammingtons are a sweet dessert. Ask an adult to help you with this recipe.

What You Need

2 frozen sponge cakes
3 cups (750 mL) powdered sugar
1 cup (250 mL) of warmed milk
4 tablespoons (60 mL) cocoa
1 tablespoon (15 mL) melted butter
2 cups (500 mL) coconut

electric mixer
medium bowl
small bowl
flour sifter
large mixing spoon
measuring cups
measuring spoons
knife

What You Do

1. Sift powdered sugar and cocoa into medium bowl.
2. Mix together melted butter and warmed milk in medium bowl.
3. Pour the butter/milk mixture into the sugar/cocoa mixture. Blend with the electric mixer until smooth, or for about 3 minutes.
4. Cut the cakes into about 2-inch (5-centimeter) squares.
5. Dip each square in chocolate frosting.
6. Roll each chocolate-covered square in coconut.
7. Serve lammingtons on a plate. Store extra cakes in an airtight container.

Makes about 20 small cakes.

light lunch and a larger dinner. Australians also drink a strong, black tea, which they call "billy." Anzac biscuits are a traditional Australian snack first made for soldiers during World War I. These hard cookielike treats have a gingery taste.

Other Australian foods have a British influence. They include pumpkin scones and lammingtons. Pumpkin scones are small, flat cakes made with pumpkin. Lammingtons are sponge cakes cut into small cubes and dipped in chocolate and coconut.

Some Australians are becoming interested in bush tucker dishes. These meals use plants and animals found in the bush. Kangaroo and crocodile meat is roasted over coals. Snakes, lizards, and birds may be eaten raw. These people also eat native grasses and roots.

Clothing

Most Australians dress in styles very similar to styles in North America and Europe. They wear jeans, t-shirts, slacks, shirts, skirts, blouses, and dresses.

In the Outback, people wear clothes that stand up to the weather conditions. Station workers often wear a slouch hat called an akubra. These workers also wear oilskin coats to protect themselves against rain. These coats are made of oiled cotton to repel water. Workers

also wear large shoulder capes that allow rain to run off the back instead of down the neck.

Aborigines who live in tribal areas sometimes wear a loincloth called a naga for ceremonies. The cloth hangs from the waist. Today, most Aborigines' everyday dress is western clothing.

▲ This farmer wears an akubra and an oilskin coat with shoulder capes.

Australian Art and Literature

Australia has many talented artists and enjoys art forms that are unique to Australian culture. Adventurous poems set in the Australian Outback, called "bush ballads," became popular in the 1890s. "Waltzing Matilda" is an example of a famous bush ballad.

"Once a jolly swagman camped by a billabong, Under the shade of a coolibah tree, And he sang as he watched and waited 'til his billy boiled, "Who'll come a-waltzing, Matilda, with me?"

–First verse of "Waltzing Matilda"

Today, Australians write novels and stories about city life as well as life in the bush. Australian writer Patrick White (1912–1990) won the 1973 Nobel Prize for literature. His works about Australian life include *The Tree of Man* and *The Eye of the Storm*. Aborigines have an artistic tradition that dates back long before European arrival. They paint very detailed human and animal figures on bark and rock.

Sports and Recreation

Australians enjoy many relaxing activities. They visit with friends, go for walks, and watch television. Families especially enjoy relaxing outdoors and cooking on their "barbie," an Australian word for barbecue grill.

▼ Modern Aboriginal artists sometimes paint on cloth.

Outdoor sports are very popular in sunny Australia. Many Australians enjoy water activities such as diving, surfing, swimming, or boating. Some play golf or tennis. Team sports such as cricket are extremely popular in Australia. Cricket is an English game played with bats and a ball. The most famous Australian sporting event is the Melbourne Cup, a yearly horse race that attracts fans from around the world.

Australians enjoy various team games. Rugby is a type of football invented in England. Australia has two professional rugby leagues. Australians play their own style of football called Australian Rules football, or "footy." The players do not wear padded protective gear. Soccer is another popular sport in Australia. It is the fastest growing team sport in Australia. Netball, a form of basketball, is the most popular sport among Australian women.

Holidays

Australians celebrate many holidays and festivals. Australia Day is on January 26. People recognize the founding of the first British colony in Australia with outdoor events and fireworks. Australians honor service workers on Boxing Day, December 26. People give money to service workers such as mail carriers and barbers who have helped them during the previous year. Anzac Day on April 25 recognizes soldiers who served in war. They are honored with parades and special military services at war memorials.

Australians celebrate other holidays as well. They observe Christian holidays such as Christmas and Easter. They also celebrate New Year's Day on January 1 and the Queen's birthday in June.

▲ Cathy Freeman wears the Australian and Aboriginal flags around her neck during her victory lap. She won the women's 400 meter dash at the 2000 Olympics in Sydney.

▲ The koala is a marsupial native only to Australia.

Australia's National Symbols

◀ **Australia's Flag**

The Australian flag was adopted in 1909. The flag is dark blue with a small British flag in the top left corner. A seven-pointed star is beneath the small flag. Six points of the star stand for the six states and one point represents the territories. Five seven-pointed stars, which stand for the stars in the star formation called the Southern Cross, are located on the right side of the flag.

◀ **Australia's Coat of Arms**

Australia's coat of arms shows a shield supported by a kangaroo and an emu. The kangaroo and emu are the national animals. The shield is divided into six areas. Each area contains a different state's symbol. The shield is supported on a golden wattle branch. Wattle is Australia's floral emblem.

Other National Symbols

National animals: kangaroo and emu

National anthem: "Advance Australia Fair"

National colors: green and gold

National flower emblem: golden wattle

National gemstone: opal

Timeline

1801
Matthew Flinders sails around Australia, proving it to be an island.

1770
James Cook claims Australia's east coast for Great Britain.

1851
Gold is discovered in New South Wales and Victoria.

A.D. 1606
Willem Jansz lands in Australia.

B.C.   A.D. 1600   1800

48,000 B.C.
Aborigines begin to settle in Australia.

1642
Abel Janszoon Tasman sights Van Dieman's Land.

1788
Great Britain establishes a prison colony in New South Wales.

1829
Charles Freemantle claims Western Australia for Great Britain.

1993
Native Title
Act is passed;
Aborigines
and Torres
Strait
Islanders can
make claim to
tribal lands.

1967
The Australian
Constitution is
amended to
make Aborigines
citizens.

1901
Australia
becomes a
federation.

1900   **1950**   **2000**

1868
Britain ends
transportation
to most of
Australia.

1927
Federal capital
is transferred
to Canberra.

1978
The Northern
Territory gains
self-government.

Words to Know

Aborigines (ab-uh-RIJ-uh-neez)—one of the native peoples of Australia

bush (BUSH)—Australia's countryside

eucalyptus (yoo-kuh-LIP-tuhss)—a fragrant evergreen tree that grows in dry climates

joey (JOH-ee)—a young kangaroo

marsupial (mar-SOO-pee-uhl)—an animal that carries its young in a pouch on its abdomen

Outback (OUT-bak)—the remote, sparsely populated countryside of Australia

snorkeling (SNOR-kuhl-ing)—underwater swimming while breathing through a tube; people snorkel to view the Great Barrier Reef.

station (STAY-shuhn)—a large cattle or sheep ranch

Torres Strait Islanders (TOR-iz STRAYT EYE-lunhd-ers)—a native group of Australia that settled on islands off Australia's northeast coast

transportation (transs-pur-TAY-shuhn)—the practice of shipping criminals to a far-off colony; Britain practiced transportation by sending criminals to colonies in Australia.

To Learn More

Bartlett, Anne. *The Aboriginal Peoples of Australia.* First Peoples. Minneapolis: Lerner, 2002.

Darlington, Robert. *Australia.* Nations of the World. Austin, Texas: Raintree-Steck Vaughn, 2001.

Finley, Carol. *Aboriginal Art of Australia: Exploring Cultural Traditions.* Art around the World. Minneapolis: Lerner, 1999.

Gutnik, Martin J., and Natalie Browne-Gutnik. *Great Barrier Reef.* Wonders of the World. Austin, Texas.: Raintree-Steck Vaughn, 1995.

Heinrichs, Ann. *Australia.* Enchantment of the World. New York: Children's Press, 1998.

Sayre, April Pulley. *Australia.* The Seven Continents. Brookfield, Conn.: Twenty-First Century Books, 1998.

Stein, R. Conrad. *Sydney*. Cities of the World. New York: Children's Press, 1998.

Useful Addresses

Australia High Commission

7th Floor, Suite 710

50 O' Connor Street

Ottawa, Ontario   K1P 6L2

Canada

Embassy of Australia

1601 Massachusetts Avenue NW

Washington, DC 20036

Internet Sites

Adventure 2000 Down Under

http://www.famie.com/australia/kids.htm

Geography, people, government, wildlife, and much more

Australia in Focus

http://www.pm.gov.au/aust_focus/index.htm

Australian statistics, symbols, government, and other information

CIA—The World Factbook (Australia)

http://www.cia.gov/cia/publications/factbook/geos/as.html

Information from the U.S. Central Intelligence Agency

Embassy of Australia

http://www.austemb.org

Contains statistics, travel information, and a kids page about Australia

▲ Australia is ranked eighth in world grape production.

Index